This edition first published in the UK by Scholastic, 2024
1 London Bridge, London, SE1 9BG
Scholastic Ireland, 89E Lagan Road, Dublin Industrial Estate, Glasnevin, Dublin, D11 HP5F

The Wonky Donkey first published in New Zealand by Scholastic New Zealand Limited, 2009
First published in the UK by Scholastic, 2018
The Dinky Donkey first published in New Zealand by Scholastic New Zealand Limited, 2019
First published in the UK by Scholastic, 2019
The Grinny Granny Donkey first published in New Zealand by Scholastic New Zealand Limited, 2020
First published in the UK by Scholastic, 2020

First published by Scholastic New Zealand Limited.
This edition published by arrangement with Scholastic
New Zealand Limited.

ISBN 978 0702 33473 3

A CIP catalogue record for this book is available from the British Library.

Printed in China
Paper made from wood grown in sustainable forests and other controlled sources.

1 3 5 7 9 10 8 6 4 2

www.scholastic.co.uk

The Dinky Donkey Treasury

Words by Craig Smith

Illustrations by Katz Cowley

SCHOLASTIC

For my mum,
and all the people who have helped me
over the years: family, friends and mentors.
Thank you.
– Craig Smith

To my precious Mum, Dad and aunt Wren ...
your love, support and inspiration fuels my creative journey
and makes all of me smile and sing. With big-fat gratitude
for keeping me tuned to the magic and humour of life.
– Katz Cowley

The Wonky Donkey

I was walking down the road
and I saw ...

a donkey,

Hee Haw!

And he only had three legs!

He was a
wonky donkey.

I was walking down the road
and I saw a donkey,

Hee Haw!

He only had three legs ...

and one eye!

He was a **winky** wonky donkey.

I was walking down the road
and I saw a donkey,

Hee Haw!

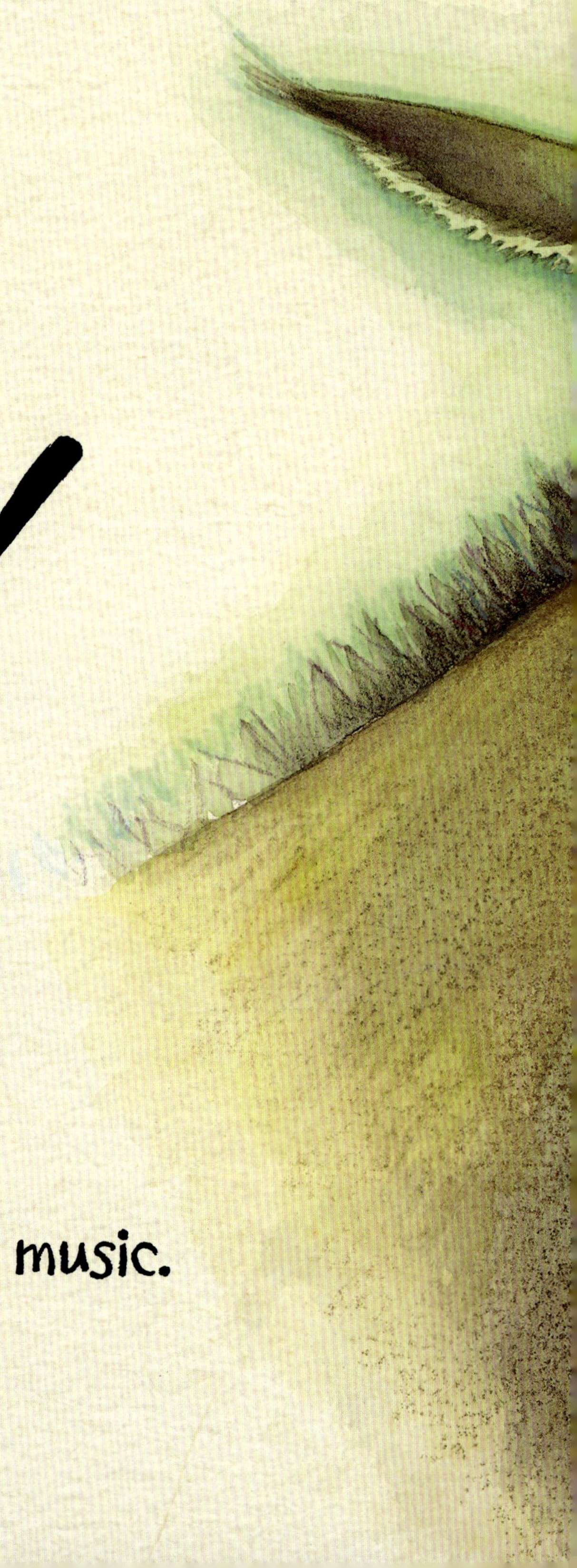

He only had three legs,
one eye ...

and he liked to listen to country music.

He was a **honky-tonky**
winky wonky donkey.

I was walking down the road
and I saw a donkey,

Hee Haw!

He only had three legs,
one eye,
he liked to listen to country music ...

and he was quite tall and slim.

He was
a **lanky**
honky-
tonky
winky
wonky
donkey.

I was walking down the road
and I saw a donkey,

Hee Haw!

He only had three legs,
one eye,
he liked to listen to country music,
he was quite tall and slim ...

and he smelt really, really bad.

He was a **stinky-dinky**
lanky honky-tonky
winky wonky donkey.

I was walking down the road
and I saw a donkey,

Hee Haw!

He only had three legs,
one eye,
he liked to listen to country music,
he was quite tall and slim,
he smelt really, really bad ...

**and that morning he'd got up early
and hadn't had any coffee.**

He was a **cranky**
stinky-dinky lanky
honky-tonky
winky wonky donkey.

I was walking down the road
and I saw a donkey,

Hee Haw!

He only had three legs,
one eye,
he liked to listen to country music,
he was quite tall and slim,
he smelt really, really bad,
that morning he'd got up early
and hadn't had any coffee ...

and he was always getting up to mischief.

He was a **hanky-panky** cranky stinky-dinky
lanky honky-tonky winky wonky donkey.

I was walking down the road
and I saw a donkey,

Hee Haw!

He only had three legs,
one eye,
he liked to listen to country music,
he was quite tall and slim,
he smelt really, really bad,
that morning he'd got up early
and hadn't had any coffee,
he was always getting up to mischief ...

but he was quite good looking!

He was a **spunky** hanky-panky cranky
stinky-dinky lanky honky-tonky winky wonky donkey!

I was walking down the road

and I saw a donkey ...

Heee

Howw!

For Maia. My beautiful girl.

– Craig Smith

To the gorgeously giggling Scottish Granny, who has touched hearts across the globe with her laughter medicine, reading to the adorable Archer and inspiring reading aloud to children worldwide.

And to Felicity . . . for being sent from heaven.

– Katz Cowley

The Dinky Donkey

Wonky Donkey had a child ...

it was a little girl.

Hee Haw!

She was so cute and small!

She was a **dinky** donkey.

Wonky Donkey had a child,
it was a little girl.

Hee Haw!

She was so cute and small ...

and she had beautiful *long* eyelashes!

She was a
blinky dinky
donkey.

Wonky Donkey had a child,
it was a little girl.

Hee Haw!

She was so cute and small,
she had beautiful long eyelashes ...

and she loved to listen to rowdy music.

She was a **punky** blinky dinky donkey.

Wonky Donkey had a child,
it was a little girl.

Hee Haw!

She was so cute and small,
she had beautiful long eyelashes,
she loved to listen to rowdy music ...

and she painted her hooves bright pink.

She was an
inky-pinky
punky
blinky
dinky donkey.

Wonky Donkey had a child,
it was a little girl.

Hee Haw!

She was so cute and small,
she had beautiful long eyelashes,
she loved to listen to rowdy music,
she painted her hooves bright pink ...

and she had to go pee-pee.

She was a **winky-tinky** inky-pinky
punky blinky dinky donkey.

Wonky Donkey had a child,
it was a little girl.

Hee Haw!

She was so cute and small,
she had beautiful long eyelashes,
she loved to listen to rowdy music,
she painted her hooves bright pink,
she had to go pee-pee ...

and she loved to play the piano.

She was a **plinky-plonky**
winky-tinky inky-pinky
punky blinky dinky donkey.

Wonky Donkey had a child,
it was a little girl.

Hee Haw!

She was so cute and small,
she had beautiful long eyelashes,
she loved to listen to rowdy music,
she painted her hooves bright pink,
she had to go pee-pee,
she loved to play the piano ...

and she wore wild sunglasses.

She was a **funky** plinky-plonky winky-tinky
inky-pinky punky blinky dinky donkey.

Wonky Donkey had a child,
it was a little girl.

Hee Haw!

She was so cute and small,
she had beautiful long eyelashes,
she loved to listen to rowdy music,
she painted her hooves bright pink,
she had to go pee-pee,
she loved to play the piano,
she wore wild sunglasses ...

and she smelt just as **bad**
as her dad.

She was a **stinky** funky plinky-plonky winky-tinky
inky-pinky punky blinky dinky donkey.

Wonky Donkey had a child,

it was a little girl ...

Hee Hee
Hee Haw!

For Fiona, Archer and the original Grinny Granny herself,
Janice Clark. You will forever make me smile.
And for all the grandparents who sing and
read to their grandchildren.
– Craig Smith

To Archer, may you always be filled with endless love and giggles,
and may you never forget that you have a marvellously magical
Scottish Granny who has melted hearts all over the world.
– Katz Cowley

The Grinny Granny Donkey

There was a sweet donkey
who lived on the heath.

She was so funny
with her false teeth ...

Hee Haw!

But her teeth kept falling out!

She was a
clunky donkey.

There was a sweet donkey who lived on the heath.
She was so funny with her false teeth ...

Hee Haw!

But her teeth kept falling out!

She loved to sip her favourite brew
and dunk her biscuits in it.

She was a
dunky-drinky,
clunky donkey.

There was a sweet donkey who lived on the heath.
She was so funny with her false teeth ...

Hee Haw!

But her teeth kept falling out!

She loved to sip her favourite brew,
dunk her biscuits in it ...

and fall asleep in the afternoon sun.

She was a **zonky,**
dunky-drinky,
clunky donkey.

There was a sweet donkey who lived on the heath.
She was so funny with her false teeth ...

Hee Haw!

But her teeth kept falling out!

She loved to sip her favourite brew,
dunk her biscuits in it,
fall asleep in the afternoon sun ...

then go for walks with her jewellery on.

She was a **clinky-clanky**, zonky,
dunky-drinky, clunky donkey.

There was a sweet donkey who lived on the heath.
She was so funny with her false teeth ...

Hee Haw!

But her teeth kept falling out!

She loved to sip her favourite brew,
dunk her biscuits in it,
fall asleep in the afternoon sun,
go for walks with her jewellery on ...

and she always dressed smartly.

She was a **swanky**,
clinky-clanky, zonky,
dunky-drinky,
clunky donkey.

There was a sweet donkey who lived on the heath.
She was so funny with her false teeth ...

Hee Haw!

But her teeth kept falling out!

She loved to sip her favourite brew,
dunk her biscuits in it,
fall asleep in the afternoon sun,
go for walks with her jewellery on,
dress smartly ...

and she played her banjo to relax.

She was a
plunky-plinky,
swanky,
clinky-clanky,
zonky,
dunky-drinky,
clunky donkey.

There was a sweet donkey who lived on the heath.
She was so funny with her false teeth ...

Hee Haw!

But her teeth kept falling out!

She loved to sip her favourite brew,
dunk her biscuits in it,
fall asleep in the afternoon sun,
go for walks with her jewellery on,
dress smartly and play her banjo to relax ...

**BUT if she hadn't had a visit from her family
in a while, she would sometimes get grumpy and cranky!**

She was a **granky**,
plunky-plinky,
swanky,
clinky-clanky,
zonky,
dunky-drinky,
clunky donkey.

There was a sweet donkey who lived on the heath.
She was so funny with her false teeth ...

Hee Haw!

But her teeth kept falling out!

She loved to sip her favourite brew, dunk her biscuits in it, fall asleep in the afternoon sun, go for walks with her jewellery on, dress smartly, play her banjo to relax, and sometimes she got grumpy and cranky ...

BUT when her son Wonky turned up with her cute granddaughter Dinky, that granky granny donkey got so many cuddles and kisses that she couldn't get the smile off her face for weeks!

She was a **grinny granny**, plunky-plinky, swanky,
clinky-clanky, zonky, dunky-drinky, clunky donkey.

There was a **GRINNY GRANNY** donkey who lived on the heath. She smiled so much you could see her false teeth ...

GG ♥ WD
DD

Hee Haw!